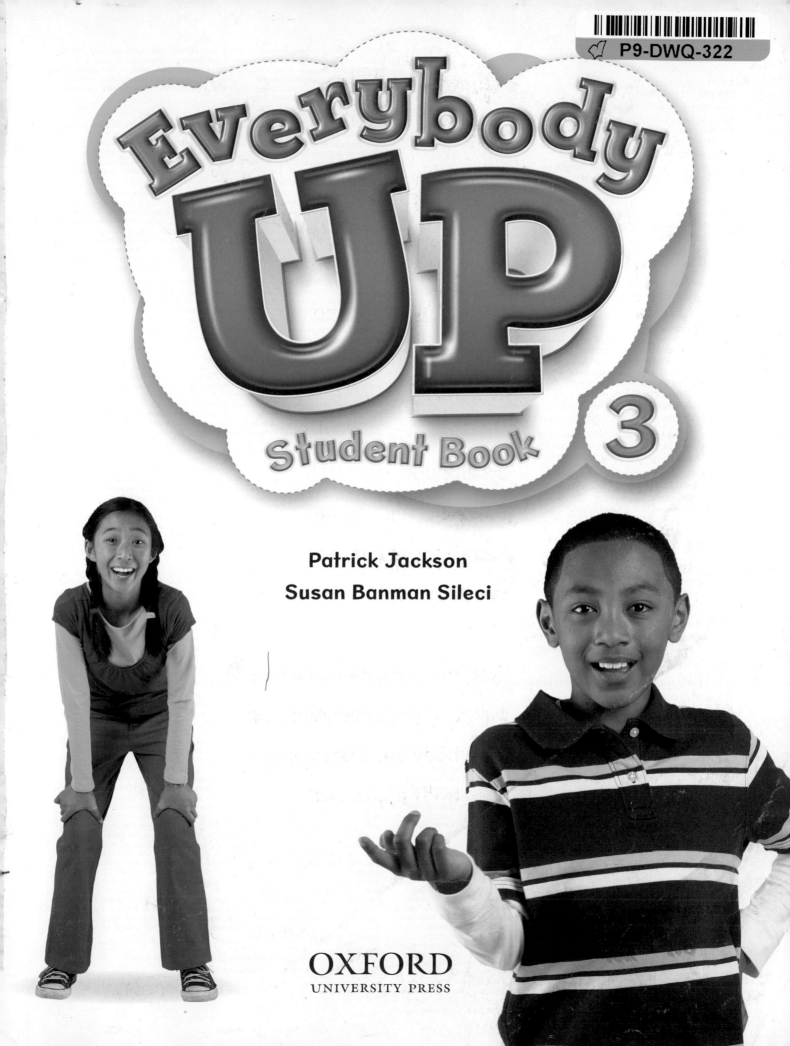

Everybody UP

Student Book 3

Patrick Jackson
Susan Banman Sileci

OXFORD
UNIVERSITY PRESS

OXFORD
UNIVERSITY PRESS

198 Madison Avenue
New York, NY 10016 USA

Great Clarendon Street, Oxford OX2 6DP UK

Oxford University Press is a department of the University of Oxford.
It furthers the University's objective of excellence in research, scholarship,
and education by publishing worldwide in

Oxford New York

Auckland Cape Town Dar es Salaam Hong Kong Karachi
Kuala Lumpur Madrid Melbourne Mexico City Nairobi
New Delhi Shanghai Taipei Toronto

With offices in

Argentina Austria Brazil Chile Czech Republic France Greece
Guatemala Hungary Italy Japan Poland Portugal Singapore
South Korea Switzerland Thailand Turkey Ukraine Vietnam

OXFORD and OXFORD ENGLISH are registered trademarks of
Oxford University Press in certain countries.

© Oxford University Press 2012

Database right Oxford University Press (maker)

No unauthorized photocopying

All rights reserved. No part of this publication may be reproduced, stored in a retrieval system, or transmitted, in any form or by any means, without the prior permission in writing of Oxford University Press, or as expressly permitted by law, or under terms agreed with the appropriate copyright clearance organization. Enquiries concerning reproduction outside the scope of the above should be sent to the ELT Rights Department, Oxford University Press, at the address above.

You must not circulate this book in any other binding or cover and you must impose this same condition on any acquirer.

Any websites referred to in this publication are in the public domain and their addresses are provided by Oxford University Press for information only. Oxford University Press disclaims any responsibility for the content.

General Manager, American ELT: Laura Pearson
Excutive Publishing Manager: Shelagh Speers
Managing Editor: Clare Hambly
Senior Development Editor: Jennifer Wos
Art, Design, and Production Director: Susan Sanguily
Design Manager: Lisa Donovan
Senior Designer: Molly K. Scanlon
Designer: Sangeeta E. Ramcharan
Image Manager: Trisha Masterson
Image Editor: Fran Newman
Production Coordinator: Hila Ratzabi
Senior Manufacturing Controller: Eve Wong

ISBN: 978-0-19-410355-8 Student Book with Audio CD
ISBN: 978-0-19-410356-5 Student Book as pack component
ISBN: 978-0-19-410357-2 Audio CD as pack component

Printed in China

This book is printed on paper from certified and well-managed sources.

10 9 8 7 6 5

ACKNOWLEDGMENTS

Oxford University Press would like to thank the thousands of teachers whose opinions helped to inform this series, and in particular, the following reviewers::

Ayoub Ait Ali, Ministry of Education, Casablanca, Morocco; **Michael P. Bassett**, Osaka International School, Minoh, Japan; **Paul Richard Batt**, Elephant's Memory Learning Institute, Taichung; **Jawida Ben Afia**, The Ministry of Education and Training, Tunis, Tunisia; **Dana Buck**, Margaret Institute of Language, Sakura, Japan; **Roberta Calderbank**, Bahrain Ministry of Education, Bahrain; **Cherry Chao**, Glory English Cram School, Taichung; **Whosiuk Che**, Hankuk University of Foreign Students, Seoul, South Korea; **Yuwen Catherine Chen**, Eden Language Institute, Taichung; **Cláudia Colla de Amorim**, Escola Móbile, São Paulo, Brazil; **Debbie Chung**, International Graduate School of English, Seoul, South Korea; **Simon R. Downes**, Simon Bear School, Tokyo, Japan; **Elaine Elia**, Escola Caminho Aberto, São Paulo, Brazil; **Mark Evans**, Wisdom Bank Language School, Kaohsiung; **Sean Gallagher**, Happy English Club, Inc., Nagoya, Japan; **Patricia Gazzi**, Christo Rei School, São Paulo, Brazil; **Kyla KCW Huang**, Kang Ning English School, Jhudong; **Keith Grehan**, Mosaica Education, Abu Dhabi, United Arab Emirates; **Anna Han**, American City Language School, Youngin, South Korea; **Briony Hewitt**, ILA Vietnam, Ho Chi Minh City, Vietnam; **Kelly Hsu**, Kelly English School, Tainan; **Janet Im**, Boston Campus, Seoul, South Korea; **Aaron Jolly**, Hanseo University, Haemi-myun and Seosan-shi, South Korea; **Sandra Katsuda**, Colégio Montessori Santa Terezinha, São Paulo, Brazil; **Sean Kim**, Kangseo Wonderland, Seoul, South Korea; **Charlotte Lee**, Jordan's Language School, Taipei; **Lilian Itzicovitch Leventhal**, Colegio I.L. Peretz, São Paulo, Brazil; **Moy Liddel**, Yonsei ELP, Wonju, South Korea; **Hsiang-pao Lin**, Lincoln International Language School, Tainan; **David Martin**, Busy Beavers English Academy, Gwangju, South Korea; **Conrad Matsumoto**, Conrad's English House, Odawara, Japan; **Daniel McNeill**, Yokohama YMCA, Yokohama, Japan; **Grace Oliviera**, Colégio Franciscano Nossa Senhora Aparecida, São Paulo, Brazil; **Gina Park**, English Bug, Anyang City, South Korea; **Juliana Queiroz Pereira**, Colégio Marista Arquidiocesano & Colégio I. L. Peretz, São Paulo, Brazil; **Saba'a Mansour Qhabi**, University of Qatar, Doha, Qatar; Karyna Ribeiro, Colégio Miguel de Cervantes, São Paulo, Brazil; **Charles Owen Richards**, The Learning Tree English School, Osaka, Japan; **Mark Riley**, Shane English School, Taipei; **John Sanders**, Camelot English Study Centre, Tokyo, Japan; **Kaj Schwermer**, Eureka Learning Institute, Osaka, Japan; **Monika Soens Yang**, Taipei European School, Taipei; **Jiyeon Song**, Seoul, South Korea; **Jason Stewart**, Taejeon International Language School, Taejeon, South Korea; **David Stucker**, Myojo Elementary School, Beppu, Japan; **Jeffrey Taschner**, AUA Language Center, Bangkok, Thailand; **Andrew Townshend**, Natural English School, Tokyo, Japan; **Thanaphong Udomsab**, ECC, Bangkok, Thailand; **Rachel Um**, Mokdong Oedae Language Institute, Seoul, South Korea; **Aliete Mara Ventura**, Escola Carandá, São Paulo, Brazil; **Ariel Yao**, Ren Da English School, Taipei.

Cover Design: Molly K. Scanlon

Illustrations by: Scott Angle: 9, 20 (middle), 21, 27, 32, 33, 40 (top), 41 (top), 54-55 (scene), 63, 64 (icons), 65 (icons) ; Barb Bastian: 28 (clipboard); Charlene Chua: 2, 4, 8, 12, 16, 22, 26, 30, 31(top), 34, 40 (bottom), 41 (bottom), 44, 48 (boy, girl), 52, 58, 62, 66, 70; Leslie Harrington: 6, 7, 17, 23, 36, 42(bottom), 43 (bottom), 53, 60, 61, 74 (middle), 75; Ken Gamage: 46-47 (background); John Kurtz: 15 (kid art), 31 (bottom), 37 (flag), 48 (kid art posters), 69 (kid art); Julissa Mora: 3 (bottom), 13, 24, 25, 35, 49, 56 (middle), 57, 71; Jomike Tejido: 5, 10, 14, 15, 28, 29, 38 (middle), 39, 45, 50, 51, 59; Sam Ward: 3 (calendar), 42 (top), 43 (top), 46 (spots), 55 (chart spots), 67, 68, 69.

Commissioned photography by: Richard Hutchings/Digital Light Source, Cover photos and all photos of kids in lower right hand corner of pages: 5, 7, 9, 11, 13, 15 and 17, four photos of the girl on page 18, all photos on page 19, girl on top of page 21, all photos of kids in lower right hand corner of pages 23, 25, 27, 29, 31, 33, 35 and 37, boy gesturing to himself on top of page 39, all photos of kids in lower right hand corner of pages 41, 43, 45, 47, 49, 51, 53 and 55, girl on top of page 57, all photos of kids in lower right hand corner of pages 59, 61, 63, 65, 67, 69, 71 and 73, and boy on top of page 75; Gareth Boden, pg. 5 (girl with braids, boy in red shirt); pg. 14 (shop); pg. 18 (color, cut, glue, fold); pg. 20 (hands folding pager); pg. 64 (blonde girl); Dennis Kitchen Studio, Inc., pg. 68 (pencil sharpener); pg. 74. (pencil sharpener) and Mark Mason, pg. 5 (chocolate); pgs. 10 & 20 (plate for omelet); pg. 11 (milk).

The publishers would like to thank the following for their kind permission to reproduce photographs: ALAMY: Chris Howes/Wild Places Photography, pg.56 (sweeping); Vittorio Sciosia, pg.59 (girl at hotel); David L. Moore, pg.60 (book store); Goss Images, pg.60 (pharmacy); British Retail Photography, pg.60 (toy store), pg.61 (bookstore), pg.74 (toy store); imagebroker, pg.61 (pharmacy); TOM MARESCHAL, pgs.64 & 74 (rainy); David L. Moore, pg.74 (book store). CORBIS: Beau Lark, pg.60 (coffee shop). GETTY IMAGES: Antenna, pg.22 (salesperson); Silvia Otte/Photonica, pg.23 (salesperson); Spyros Bourboulis/ First Light, pg.23 (vet); Bambu Productions/Iconica, pg.24 (sell things); David Young-Wolff, pgs.48 & 56 (make bed); Marc Debnam, pg.48 (clean room); Jupiterimages/Foodpix, pg.48 (set the table); Pauline St. Denis, pg.50 (taking out trash); Digital Vision/Photodisc, pg.50 (vacuuming); Jose Luis Pelaez, pg.59 (boy at amusement park); Ron Levine/The Image Bank, pg.59 (girl at museum); FRANCIS MILLER/ Time & Life Pictures, pg.72 (room-size computer). ISTOCKPHOTO: Chepe Nicoli, pg.4 (peanuts); Floortje, pg.4 (chocolate); Jbryson, pg.5 (girl 4); YinYang, pg.5 (movie popcorn); mbbirdy, pg.6 & 11 (tomato); Elnur Amikishiyev, pgs.10 & 20 (omelet); AndrewFurlongPhotography, pg.10 (fruit salad); YinYang, pg.20 (movie popcorn); Chepe Nicoli, pg.20 (peanuts); Steve Luker, pg.22 (librarian); Steve Snyder, pg.22 (postal worker); Mehmet Salih Guler, pg.23 (server); alejandro Soto, pg.24 (drive busses); Catherine Yeulet, pg.25 (salesperson); Catherine Yeulet, pg.25 (vet); omergenc, pg.37 (mail stamp); alejandro Soto, pg.38 (drive busses); Steve Snyder, pg.38 (postal worker); doga yusuf dokdok, pg.48 (do laundry); doga yusuf dokdok, pg.56 (do laundry); Nikada, pg.58 (hotel); netrun78, pg.60 (florist); Paul Fries, pg.64 (cloudy); Chris Gates, pg.64 (windy); Spiderstock, pg.64 (girl 2 right); Juanmonino, pg.64 (boy 3 left); Jacom Stephens, pg.64 (boy 3 right); Nikada, pg.74 (hotel); ragsac, pg.74 (tickets). OUP PICTUREBANK: Photodisc, pg.5 (boy 5) & (girl 6); Stockbyte, pg.6 (onion) & (peppers); Ingram, pg.6 (potato); Steve Lindridge, pg.10 (eggs); Stockbyte, pg.11 (pepper); Stockbyte, pg.20 (peppers); Comstock, pg.23 (librarian); Photodisc, pg.24 (make food) & (help sick animals); Digital Vision, pg.24 (fight fires); Digital Vision, pg. 25 (pilot); Don Hammond/Design Pics, pg.25 (bus driver); Photodisc, pg.29 (thermometer); Chris King, pg.37 (classroom background); Photodisc, pg.38 (vet); Ingram, pg.46 (balloons); Photodisc, pg.50 (watering plants); Ingram, pg.56 (balloon); Photodisc, pg.58 (beach); Image Source, pg.61 (coffee shop); Ellen McKnight, pg.64 (snowy); Fuse, pg.64 (boy 1); Mike Kemp/RubberBall, pg.64 (girl 1); Graphi-Ogre, pg.64 (Turkish flag) & (Brazilian flag); David Cook/ www.blueshiftstudios.co.uk, pg.72 (laptop); Judith Collins, pg.72 (digital camera); Judith Collins, pg.74 (digital camera); Corbis / Digital Stock, pg.74 (beachfront hotels). PHOTOLIBRARY: Mark Gibson, pg.12 (Post Office). PUNCHSTOCK: pg.23 (postal worker). SHUTTERSTOCK.COM: Roman Sigaev, pg.4 (soda can); Alex Staroseltsev, pg.4 (movie popcorn); Mettus, pg.4 (potato chips); Coprid, pg.4 (chewing gum); CREATISTA, pg.5 (boy 3); Roman Sigaev, pg.5 (soda); Nikola Bilic, pg.5 (peanuts); Marc Dietrich, pg.5 (potato chips); Margaret M Stewart, pg.5 (gum); BARRI, pg.6 (carrot); Supertrooper, pg.6 (cabbage); matka_Wariatka, pg.10 (fruit smoothie); Carlos Restrepo, pg.10 (chocolate milk shake); Mushakesa, pg.11 (strawberries); Sebastian Kaulitzki, pg.11 (peach); Alex Staroseltsev, pg.11 (apple); Max Krasnov, pg.11 (orange); Gregory Gerber, pg.11 (cheese); Sklep Spozywczy, pg.12 (park); pg.12 (movie theatre); Fedor Kondratenko, pg.12 (supermarket); Yegorius, pg.12 (Department store); Lim Yong Hian, pg.12 (library); Deklofenak, pg.14 (watch a movie); Robert Kneschke, pg.14 (borrow books); Martin Valigursky, pg.14 (kick a ball); matka_Wariatka, pg.20 (fruit smoothie); Deklofenak, pg.20 (watch a movie); BARRI, pg.20 (carrot); Lim Yong Hian, pg.20 (library); Yegorius, pg.20 (Department store); Karin Hildebrand Lau, pg.21 (movie theatre); Darren Brode pg.21 (popcorn); Lisa F. Young, pg.22 (cashier); AVAVA, pg.22 (server); Gelpi, pg.22 (vet); Carlos E. Santa Maria, pg.24 (fly planes); visi. stock, pg.25 (cook); Orange Line Media, pg.25 (firefighter); Angelika Krikava, pg.29 (ice pack); Niki Crucillo, pg.29 (tissue box); IngridHS, pg.29 (cup of tea); Tatiana Popova, pg.32 (fork, knife and spoon); KULISH VIKTORIIA, pg.32 (plate); Liviu Toader, pg.32 (bowl); VanHart, pg.32 (cup); Jelica Videnovic, pg.36 (Mexico); Stephen Finn, pg.36 (Japan); Aelius Aaron, pg.36 (Russia); Adem Demir, pg.36 (Turkey); djdarkflower, pg.36 (air-mail); stocksnapp, pgs.36-37 (Mail stamps from around the world); Jacek Chabraszewski, pg.37 (kids holding poster); Tatiana Popova, pg.38 (spoon); Jelica Videnovic, pg.38 (Mexico); Adem Demir, pg.38 (Turkey); KULISH VIKTORIIA, pg.38 (plate); AVAVA, pg.38 (server); JHDT Stock Images LLC, pg.39 (cousins); Stephen Aaron Rees, pg.46 (rock); Baloncici, pg.46 (pillow); sonya etchison, pg.48 (walk the dog); qingqing, pg.48 (wash dishes); MANDY GODBEHEAR, pg.50 (washing the car); Stephen Aaron Rees, pg.56 (rock); Yuri Arcurs, pg.57 (family); Bomshtein, pg.57 (cleaning supplies); BlueOrange Studio, pg.58 (aquarium); Racheal Grazias, pg.58 (amusement park); Jim Lopes, pg.58 (museum); Cheryl Casey, pg.58 (pool); Micha Rosenwirth, pg.59 (boy at beach); Mircea BEZERGHEANU, pg.59 (girl at aquarium); Juriah Mosin, pg.59 (boy at pool); Amy Walters, pg.60 (hair salon); ShutterVision, pg.61 (hair salon); ROBERT SBARRA, pg.61 (toy store); Lynn Watson, pg.61 (flower shop); Vibrant Image Studio, pg.64 (sunny); Zastol`skiy Victor Leonidovich, pg.64 (stormy); grafica, pg.64 JinYoung Lee, pg.64 R. Gino Santa Maria, pg.64 (Mexican flag); CAN BALCIOGLU, pg.64 (beach in Mexico); Hashim Pudiyapura, pg.64 (ruins in Turkey); jbor, pg.64 (San Paolo); R. Gino Santa Maria, pg.64 (South Korean flag); JinYoung Lee, pg.64 (Korean temple); Galyna Andrushko, pgs.64-65 (Green grassland and storm cloud); Leonid_tit, pgs.64-65 (grass and rainbow); Marilyn Barbone, pg. 65 (lightning); Ultrashock, pg.66 (folder); Aida Ricciardiello, pg.66 (lunch box); Smit, pg.66 (water bottle); Sebastian Crocker, pg.66 (dictionary); Christophe Testi, pg.66 (calculator); Anthony DiChello, pg.66 (stapler); Edyta Pawlowska, pg.66 (paintbrush); BonD80, pg.66 (scissors); Vasil Vasilev, Alexandr Makarov, pg.66 (glue stick); pg.72 (Motherboard PC); Ravl, pgs.72-73 (electronic circuit board); Jaroslaw Grudzinski, pg.72 (cell phone); Phase4Photography, pg.72 (flat screen TV); Marc Dietrich, pg.72 (old phone); James Steidl, pg.72 (old TV); Stephen Coburn, pg.72 (old camera); Alexandr Makarov, pg.74 (glue stick); Cheryl Casey, pg.74 (pool); Smit, pg.74 (water bottle); Phase4Photography, pg.74 (flat screen TV); Location Photography by Mannicmedia, pg. 74 (video); Zastol`skiy Victor Leonidovich, pg.74 (stormy); Ultrashock, pg.74 (folder).

Music by:
Julie Gold, Red Grammer, Troy McDonald and Devon Thagard, Ilene Weiss

For my amazing family—Riccardo, Audrey, and Natalie.

—S.B.S.

With thanks to my darling Yuko. May all your dreams come true.

—P.J.

Table of Contents

Welcome

A Listen, read, and say. CD 03

1.
> I'm a student. I'm doing my homework in my bedroom. My desk is next to my bed. My favorite subject is math. What's your favorite subject?

Julie

2.
> It's six thirty in the evening. I'm at home. I'm listening to music. We eat dinner at seven o'clock. I'm hungry. I want spaghetti! When do you eat dinner?

Mike

3.
> I'm excited! I'm playing my new video game in the living room. I like karate. I go to karate class on Mondays. When do you go to English class?

Danny

4.
> Look, purple flowers! They smell good. My favorite color is purple. I'm wearing a purple shirt and a purple skirt. I'm wearing purple shoes, too! What are you wearing?

Emma

B What about you? Talk with your classmates.

C Listen, ask, and answer. Then practice. CD1 04

What's the date today?	It's January 1st.

What's = What is
It's = It is

Sunday	Monday	Tuesday	Wednesday	Thursday	Friday	Saturday
						1st first
2nd second	**3rd** third	**4th** fourth	**5th** fifth	**6th** sixth	**7th** seventh	**8th** eighth
9th ninth	**10th** tenth	**11th** eleventh	**12th** twelfth	**13th** thirteenth	**14th** fourteenth	**15th** fifteenth
16th sixteenth	**17th** seventeenth	**18th** eighteenth	**19th** nineteenth	**20th** twentieth	**21st** twenty-first	**22nd** twenty-second
23rd twenty-third	**24th** twenty-fourth	**25th** twenty-fifth	**26th** twenty-sixth	**27th** twenty-seventh	**28th** twenty-eighth	**29th** twenty-ninth
30th thirtieth	**31st** thirty-first					

January
February
March
April
May
June
July
August
September
October
November
December

D Listen, point, and say. CD1 05

1.
Study for a test.

2.
Take a test.

3.
Check your homework.

4.
Hand in your homework.

03

3

1 Things to Eat

Lesson 1 Snacks

A Listen, point, and say. CD1 06

1	2	3	4	5	6
gum	popcorn	peanuts	chocolate	potato chips	soda

04

B Listen and find. CD1 07

C Listen and say. Then practice. CD1 08))

I want some gum.	I don't want any gum.
He / She wants some gum.	He / She doesn't want any gum.

don't = do not
doesn't = does not

1. I
2. She
3. He
4. I
5. He
6. She

D Listen, ask, and answer. Then practice. CD1 09))

What do you want?	I want some gum.
What does he / she want?	He / She wants some gum.

1. I
2. She
3. He
4. I
5. He
6. She

E Look at B. Point, ask, and answer.

What does she want?

She wants some potato chips.

I want some peanuts. What about you?

Lesson 2 **Vegetables**

A **Listen, point, and say.** 🎧 CD1 10

1	2	3	4	5	6
carrot	onion	pepper	cabbage	potato	tomato

05

B **Listen, ask, and answer. Then practice.** 🎧 CD1 11

Do you need any carrots?	Yes, we do. No, we don't.	carrots	onions	peppers
		cabbages	potatoes	tomatoes

We need:
carrots
peppers
potatoes

C Listen, ask, and answer. Then practice. CD1 12

What do they need?	They need	a carrot. some carrots.

a carrot   an onion
a pepper   a cabbage
a potato   a tomato

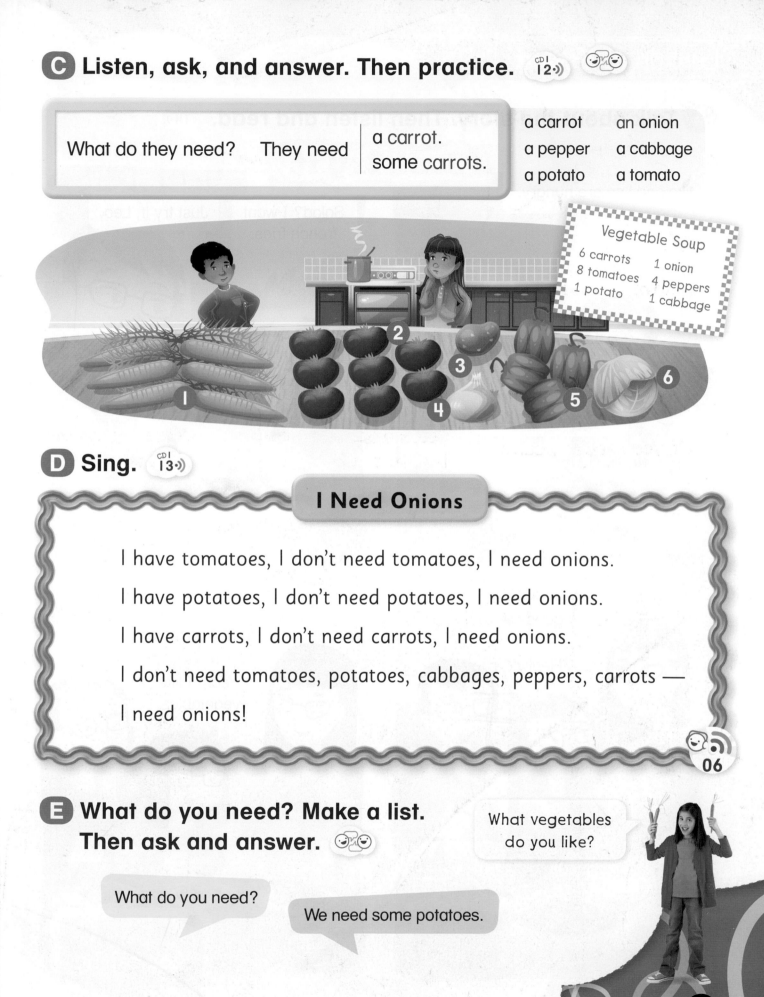

Vegetable Soup
6 carrots   1 onion
8 tomatoes   4 peppers
1 potato   1 cabbage

D Sing. CD1 13

I Need Onions

I have tomatoes, I don't need tomatoes, I need onions.

I have potatoes, I don't need potatoes, I need onions.

I have carrots, I don't need carrots, I need onions.

I don't need tomatoes, potatoes, cabbages, peppers, carrots —

I need onions!

06

E What do you need? Make a list. Then ask and answer.

What vegetables
do you like?

What do you need?

We need some potatoes.

A Talk about the story. Then listen and read.

B Read and circle.

1. Mike and Leo are hungry.   Yes   No
2. Mike likes soup and salad.   Yes   No
3. Mike and Leo's mom makes french fries.   Yes   No
4. Leo wants vegetables.   Yes   No

C Sing.

That Sounds Good

What's for breakfast?   Yogurt and an apple.

   Yogurt and an apple.   French fries, french fries.

That sounds good, but   Yogurt and an apple.

I want french fries!   Just try it!

French fries, french fries.   Mmm, it's good.

lunch
soup
salad

dinner
chicken
potatoes

07

D Listen and say. Then act.

What's for lunch?

Soup and salad.

That sounds good.

lunch: soup and salad

2
breakfast: bread and juice

3
dinner: steak and french fries

What do you want for dinner?

Lesson 4 Cooking

Health

A Listen, point, and say. CD1 17

1. omelet
2. smoothie
3. fruit salad
4. milkshake

08

B Listen and say. Then listen and read. CD1 18

I want to make an omelet.

| an omelet | a smoothie |
| a fruit salad | a milkshake |

1. I want to make an omelet. I need some eggs and some milk.

Omar

2. I want to make a smoothie. I need some bananas and some yogurt.

Ella

3. I want to make a fruit salad. I need some oranges and some peaches.

Lisa

4. I want to make a milkshake. I need some milk and some ice cream.

Tam

C Read and circle.

1.	Omar needs some bananas.	Yes	No
2.	Ella wants to make an omelet.	Yes	No
3.	Lisa needs some peaches.	Yes	No
4.	Tam wants to make a milkshake.	Yes	No

D What do you want to make? Write a list.

I want to make _____

I need _____

_____

_____

_____

_____

E Look at your list.
Talk with your classmates.

I want to make a salad.

Can you make a smoothie?

What do you need?

I need some tomatoes, some peppers, and some cheese.

2 Around Town

A Listen, point, and say. CD1 19

1	2	3	4	5	6
park	movie theater	supermarket	post office	department store	library

09

B Listen and find. CD1 20

C Listen, ask, and answer. Then practice. CD1 21 »))

Where's = Where is

> Where's the park?
>   It's across from the movie theater.

across from

1. 2. 3.

4. 5. 6.

D Listen, ask, and answer. Then practice. CD1 22 »))

> Where's the park?
>   It's between the school and the movie theater.

between

School

1 2 3 4 5 6

E Look at B. Point, ask, and answer.

> Where's the library?

> It's across from
> the post office.

> Where's your
> school?

A **Listen, point, and say.** CD1 23»

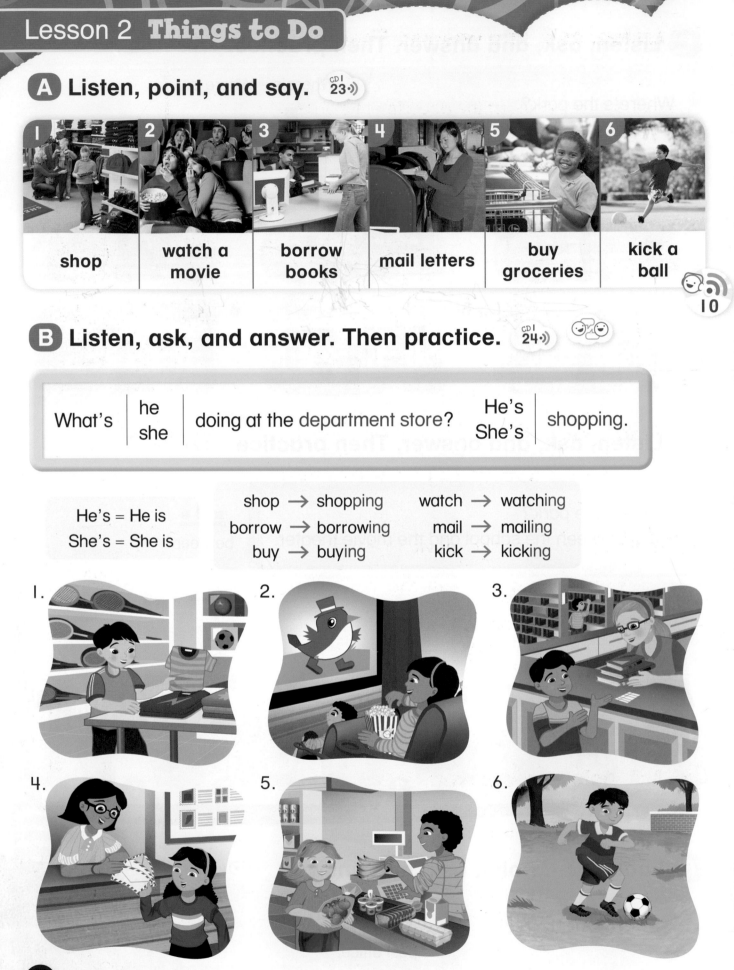

1	2	3	4	5	6
shop	watch a movie	borrow books	mail letters	buy groceries	kick a ball

10

B **Listen, ask, and answer. Then practice.** CD1 24»

| What's | he / she | doing at the department store? | He's / She's | shopping. |

He's = He is
She's = She is

shop → shopping   watch → watching
borrow → borrowing   mail → mailing
buy → buying   kick → kicking

1.

2.

3.

4.

5.

6.

C Listen, ask, and answer. Then practice. CD1 25•))

What are they doing at the department store?
   They're shopping.

They're = They are

1.
2.
3.

4.
5.
6.

D Sing. CD1 26•))

What's He Doing?

What's he doing at the movie theater?
   He's watching a movie at the movie theater.
What are they doing at the movie theater?
   They're watching a movie at the movie theater.

| she |
| library |
| borrowing books |

| he |
| post office |
| mailing letters |

E Act, ask, and answer.

What's she doing?

Where is she?

What are they doing?

She's kicking a ball.

She's at the park.

A **Talk about the story. Then listen and read.** CD1 27

B Read and circle.

1. The man is lost.   Yes   No
2. He's going to the supermarket.   Yes   No
3. James and Julie help the man.   Yes   No
4. The post office is next to the library.   Yes   No

C Sing. CD1 28

It's Over There

Excuse me. Where's the post office?

It's over there.

Ah! I see it. I see the post office.

It's over there.

restaurant

supermarket

12

D Listen and say. Then act. CD1 29

Excuse me. Where's the post office?

It's over there.

1

post office

2

park

3

school

Where's your school?

Lesson 4 Activities

Art

A Listen, point, and say. CD1 30

1	2	3	4
color	cut	glue	fold

13

B Listen and say. Then listen and read. CD1 31

First, color the house.

First → Next → Then → Finally

1. Let's make a town.
First, color the house
and buildings.
What colors
do you like?

2. Next, cut the paper.
What shapes can
you see?

3. Then, fold the paper. Can your
house stand?

4. Finally, glue the house.
Great job!

C Read and number.

1. Then, fold the paper. ____

2. Finally, glue the house. ____

3. First, color the house and buildings. ____

4. Next, cut the paper. ____

D Make a town with your classmates.

E Look at your town.
Ask and answer.

Where's the school?

It's across from the library.

The movie theater in my town is next to the supermarket.

Review 1

Award

A I can say these words.

1.
2.
3.
4.
5.
6.
7.
8.
9.
10.
11.
12.

B I can talk about these topics.

1. snacks

2. vegetables

3. cooking

4. places to go

5. things to do

6. activities

C I can talk with you.

1. What's for breakfast?

2. It's over there.

A Listen and read. (CD1 32)

Movie Day

My name is Stephanie. My friends and I go to the movie theater on Saturdays. It's between the library and the park. We like watching movies. We eat popcorn, too. It's fun!

B Read and answer.

1. What is her name? _____

2. Where do they go on Saturdays? _____

3. Where is the movie theater? _____

4. What do they eat? _____

C Listen and number. (CD1 33)

3 People in Town

A Listen, point, and say. CD1 34

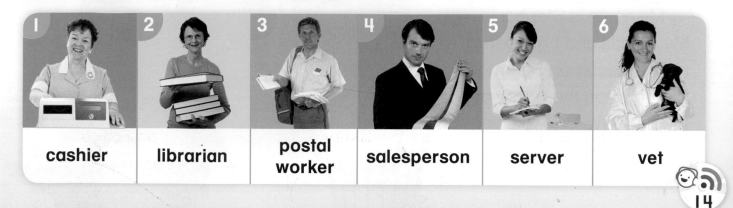

1	2	3	4	5	6
cashier	librarian	postal worker	salesperson	server	vet

B Listen and find. CD1 35

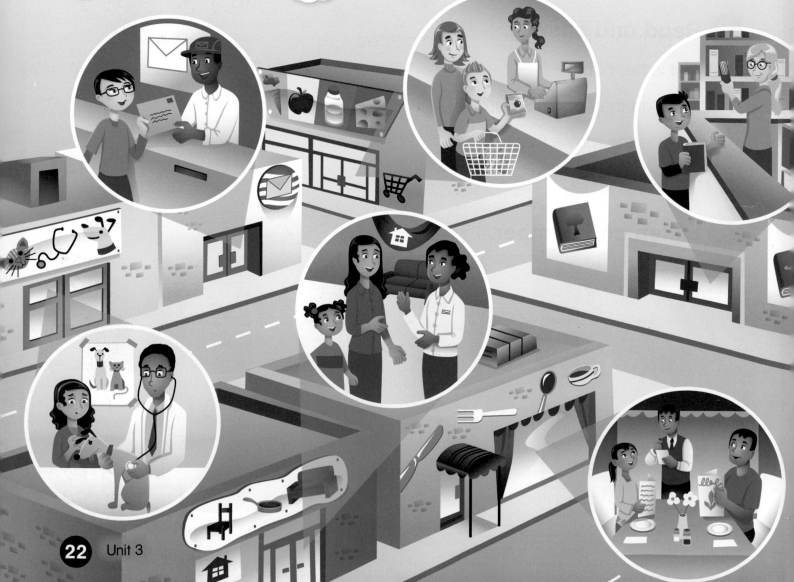

C Listen, ask, and answer. Then practice. 🎧CD1 36

> Who works at the supermarket?
> The cashier works at the supermarket.

1.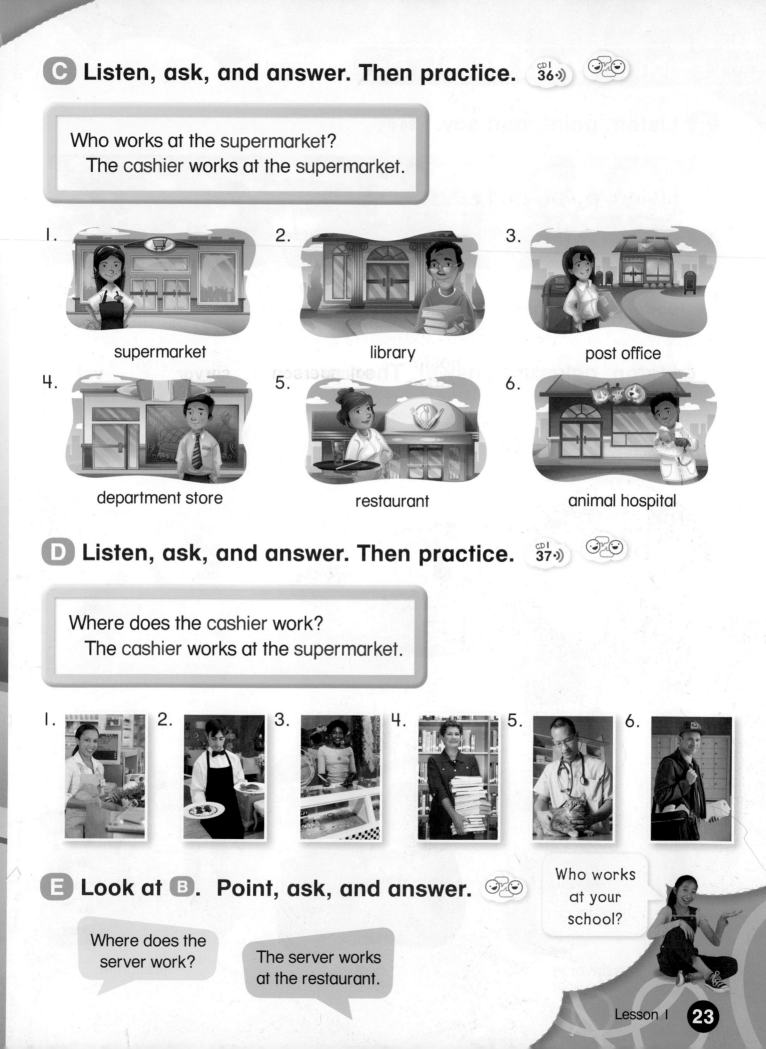
supermarket

2.
library

3.
post office

4.
department store

5.
restaurant

6.
animal hospital

D Listen, ask, and answer. Then practice. 🎧CD1 37

> Where does the cashier work?
> The cashier works at the supermarket.

1.   2.   3.   4.   5.   6.

E Look at B. Point, ask, and answer.

Who works at your school?

Where does the server work?

The server works at the restaurant.

A Listen, point, and say. CD1 38

1	2	3	4	5	6
make food	sell things	help sick animals	drive buses	fly planes	fight fires

15

B Listen, ask, and answer. Then practice. CD1 39

What does the cook do?   The cook makes food.

1. cook

2. salesperson

3. vet

4. bus driver

5. pilot

6. firefighter

C Listen, ask, and answer. Then practice. CD1 40

| Does the cook | make food? | Yes, | he | does. |
| | sell things? | No, | she | doesn't. |

1.  2. 3.

4. 5. 6.

D Listen and number. CD1 41

E What about you? Ask and answer.

What does your mother do?

Does your father drive buses?

No, he doesn't.

A Talk about the story. Then listen and read. CD1 42

B Read and circle.

1. It's Emma's birthday.   Yes   (No)
2. The sweater is $30.   (Yes)   No
3. The shoes are $15.   Yes   (No)
4. They make a sweater for Mom.   Yes   (No)

C Sing. 🎵 CD1 43

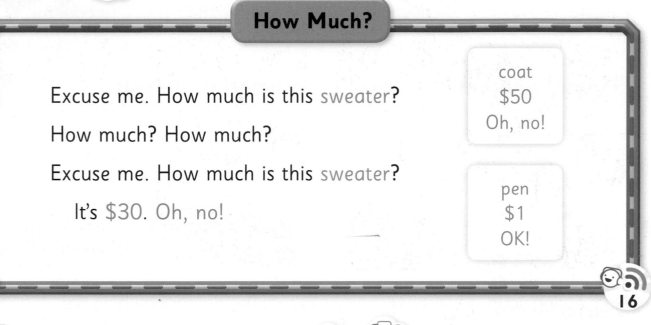

How Much?

Excuse me. How much is this sweater?

How much? How much?

Excuse me. How much is this sweater?

It's $30. Oh, no!

coat
$50
Oh, no!

pen
$1
OK!

16

D Listen and say. Then act. CD1 44

Excuse me. How much is this sweater?

It's $30.

sweater: $30

2

bike: $200

3

pen: $1

What can you make?

Lesson 4 Illnesses

Health

A Listen, point, and say. CD1 45

1. cold
2. fever
3. stomachache
4. headache

17

B Listen, ask, and answer. Then listen and read. CD1 46

| What's the matter with | him?
her? | He
She | has a cold. |

he → him
she → her

1. Matt is sick. What's the matter with him? He has a cold. He's eating soup.

2. Maggie is sick. What's the matter with her? She has a fever. The doctor can help her.

3. This is Nick. What's the matter with him? He has a stomachache. He isn't at school today.

4. This is Kelly. She's sleeping. What's the matter with her? She has a headache.

C Read and circle.

1. Who has a cold?   Nick   Matt
2. Who has a headache?   Kelly   Maggie
3. Who has a stomachache?   Nick   Kelly
4. Who has a fever?   Matt   Maggie

D Look at the picture. Fill in the chart.

	1	2	3	4	5	6	7	8
cold								
stomachache								
fever	✓							
headache								

E Look at D. Ask and answer.

What's the matter with him?

He has a fever.

I'm not sick. I'm fine!

39°C

4 Getting Together

A Listen, point, and say.

1	2	3	4	5	6
parents	grandparents	aunt	uncle	cousin	cousin

B Listen and find.

C Listen and say. Then practice. CD1 49»

| They're Danny's parents. | He's She's | Danny's cousin. |

1. 2. 3. 4. 5. 6.

D Listen, ask, and answer. Then practice. CD1 50»

| Who are they? | They're | his her | parents. | Who's | he? she? | He's his uncle. She's his aunt. |

grandparents

① parents · uncle · aunt

Me! · cousin · cousin

grandparents

④ parents · uncle · aunt ⑥ ⑤

Me! · sister

E Look at B. Point, ask, and answer.

Who's he?

He's Danny's cousin.
He likes karate.

Do you have cousins?

Lesson 2 Things on the Table

A Listen, point, and say. CD1 51

1	2	3	4	5	6
fork	knife	spoon	plate	bowl	cup

19

B Listen and say. Then practice. CD1 52

| This fork is mine. | my → mine   your → yours |
| | his → his   her → hers |

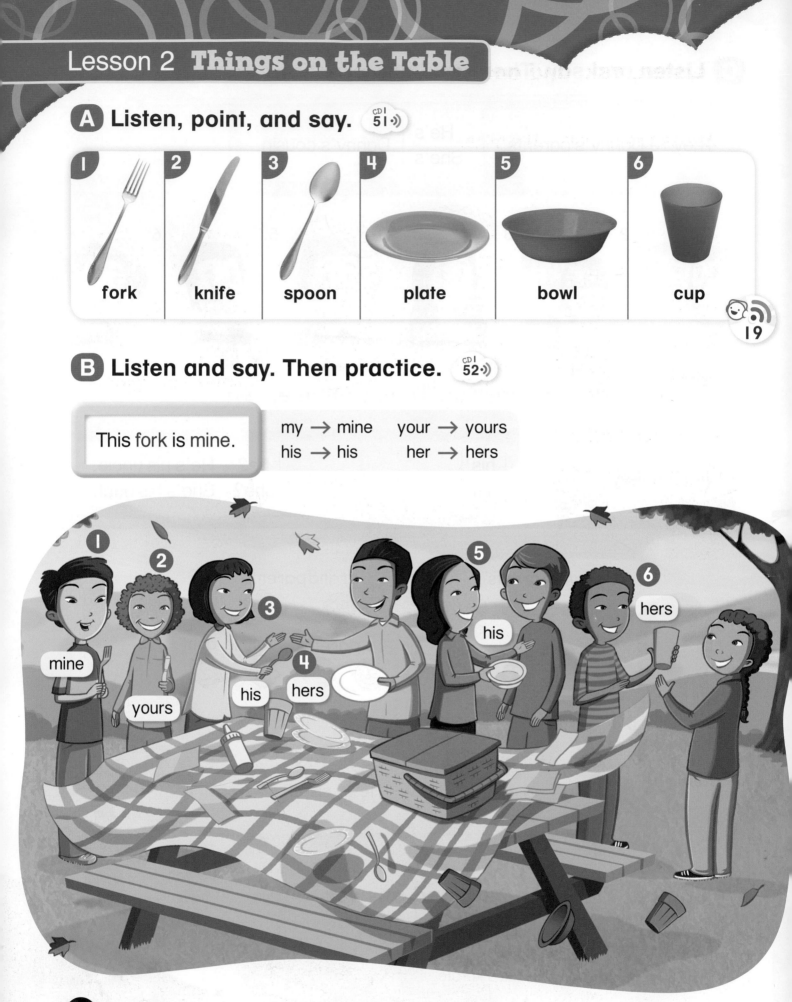

mine

yours

his

hers

his

hers

32 Unit 4

C Listen, ask, and answer. Then practice.

Whose fork is that?   It's mine.

D Listen and number.

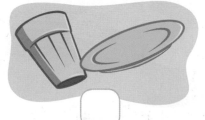

E Make cards. Ask and answer.

Whose plate is this?

It's hers.

hers

plate

Whose book is this?

A **Talk about the story. Then listen and read.** CD1 55

B Read and circle.

1. Danny and Mike are at a restaurant.   Yes   No
2. They have knives and forks.   Yes   No
3. Mike can use chopsticks.   Yes   No
4. Danny doesn't like noodles.   Yes   No

C Sing. CD1 56

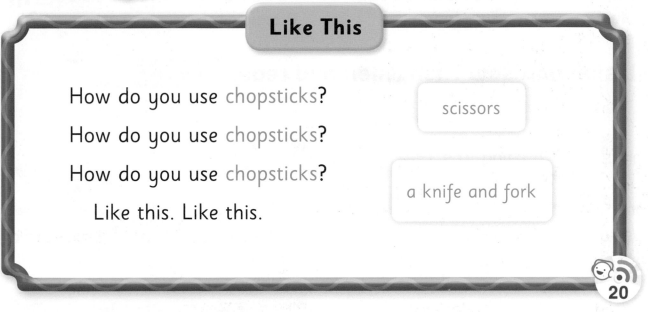

Like This

How do you use chopsticks?
How do you use chopsticks?
How do you use chopsticks?
    Like this. Like this.

scissors

a knife and fork

20

D Listen and say. Then act. CD1 57

How do you use chopsticks?

Like this.

1. chopsticks

2. a ruler

3. a computer

I can use chopsticks.

Lesson 4 Countries

Social Studies

A Listen, point, and say. 🔊 CD1 58

1. Mexico
2. Japan
3. Russia
4. Turkey 21 🔊

B Listen and say. Then listen and read. 🔊 CD1 59

| This is | our / their | flag. It's | ours. / theirs. |

our → ours
their → theirs

1. We're from Mexico. This is our flag. It's ours. It's green, white, and red.

2. We're from Japan. This is our flag. It has a red circle. It's ours.

3. They're from Russia. This is their flag. Russia's flag is white, blue, and red. It's theirs.

4. They're from Turkey. This is their flag. It's theirs. It's red and white.

C Read and circle.

1. Mexico's flag is green and blue. Yes No
2. Japan's flag has a red circle. Yes No
3. Russia's flag is blue and yellow. Yes No
4. Turkey's flag is red and white. Yes No

D Make a flag with your partner. Show and tell.

This is our flag.
It's blue and orange.

E Look at the flags. Ask and answer.

Whose flag is this?

It's theirs.

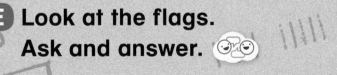

What color is your country's flag?

Review 2

A I can say these words.

1. 2. 3. 4. 5. 6.

7. 8. 9. 10. 11. 12.

B I can talk about these topics.

1. occupations

2. what people do

3. illnesses

4. family

5. things on the table

6. countries

C I can talk with you.

1. It's $200.

2. Like this.

A Listen and read. CD1 60

Our Presents

Hi, I'm Ray. These are my cousins. Their names are Josh and Sam. We're making presents for our grandparents. These are our presents. They aren't plates. They're bowls!

B Read and answer.

1. Who are Josh and Sam?

_____

2. What are they doing?

_____

3. Are they making presents for their parents?

_____

4. Are they making plates?

_____

C Listen and number. CD1 61

5 Fun in the Park

A Listen, point, and say. CD2 02

1. tall/short
2. old/young
3. strong/weak
4. girl
5. boy
6. woman
7. man

22

B Listen and find. CD2 03

C Listen and say. Then practice. CD2 04

The girl is tall.
The boy is taller.

tall	→	taller	short	→	shorter
old	→	older	young	→	younger
strong	→	stronger	weak	→	weaker

1. 2. 3. 4. 5. 6.

D Listen, ask, and answer. Then practice. CD1 05

Who's taller, Danny or Julie?
Danny is taller.

Who's = Who is

1 tall
2 short
3 old
4 young
5 strong
6 weak

E Look at B. Point, ask, and answer.

Who's older,
the man or the girl?

The man is older.

Who's taller,
you or your
friend?

Lesson 1   41

Lesson 2 Adjectives

A Listen, point, and say. CD2 06

1	2	3	4	5	6
thick	thin	clean	dirty	pretty	ugly

23

B Listen and say. Then practice. CD2 07

> The red socks are thicker than the blue socks.

thick → thicker
thin → thinner

clean → cleaner
dirty → dirtier

pretty → prettier
ugly → uglier

socks

T-shirt

hat

C Listen, ask, and answer. Then practice. CD2 08

| Is the red sweater | thicker
thinner | than the blue sweater? | Yes, it is.
No, it isn't. |

isn't = is not

1.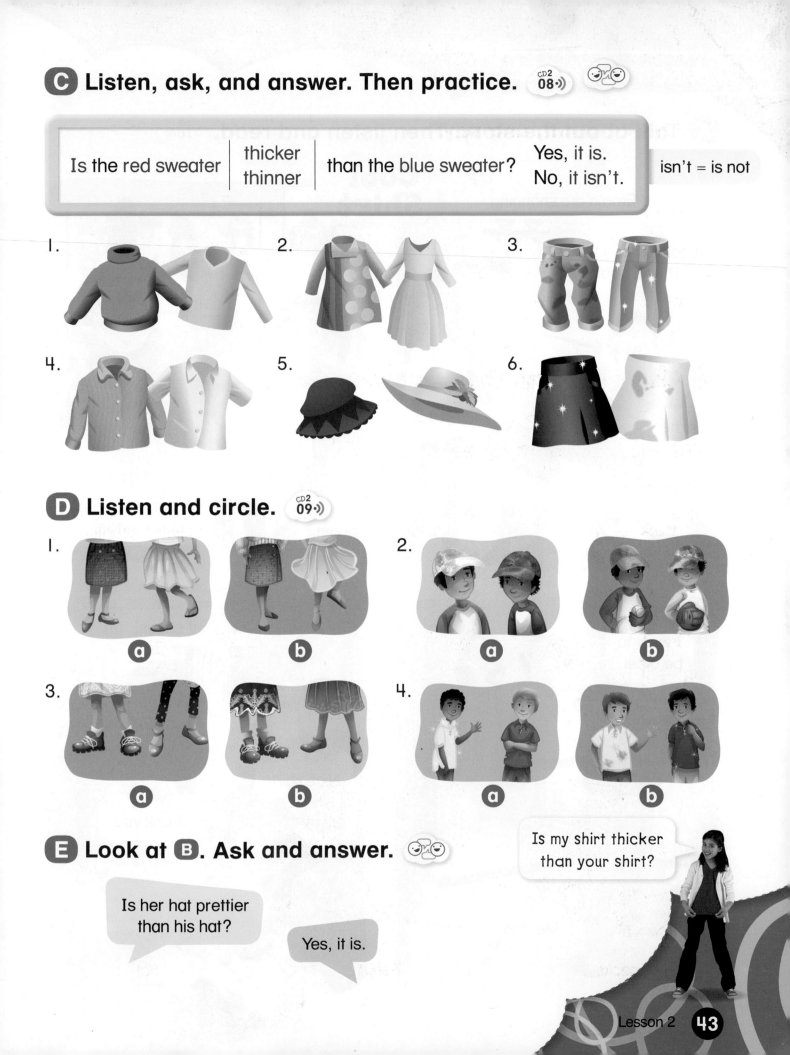

2.

3.

4.

5.

6.

D Listen and circle. CD2 09

1.
a   b

2.
a   b

3.
a   b

4.
a   b

E Look at B. Ask and answer.

Is my shirt thicker than your shirt?

Is her hat prettier than his hat?

Yes, it is.

A **Talk about the story. Then listen and read.** CD2 10

Cool Shirt

Julie and Emma are shopping.

Look at her shirt. It's so cool.

I like her boots.

I like this shirt.

We can wear cool clothes, too.

I want to be older.

Me, too!

I like your shoes!

Nice shirt!

Thank you.

Be nice.

B Read and circle.

1. Emma and Julie are in the post office. Yes   No
2. The older girls are shopping. Yes   No
3. Emma and Julie want to be younger. Yes   No
4. The older girls like Julie's shirt. Yes   No

C Sing. CD2 11))

Nice Shirt

Nice shirt! That's a cool shirt!

Thank you. Thank you.

Nice shirt! I like your shirt!

Thank you. Thank you. Thank you.

guitar

bedroom

24

D Listen and say. Then act. CD2 12))

Nice shirt!

Thank you.

shirt

bedroom

guitar

Great shoes!

Lesson 4 Adjectives

Science

A Listen, point, and say. CD2 13

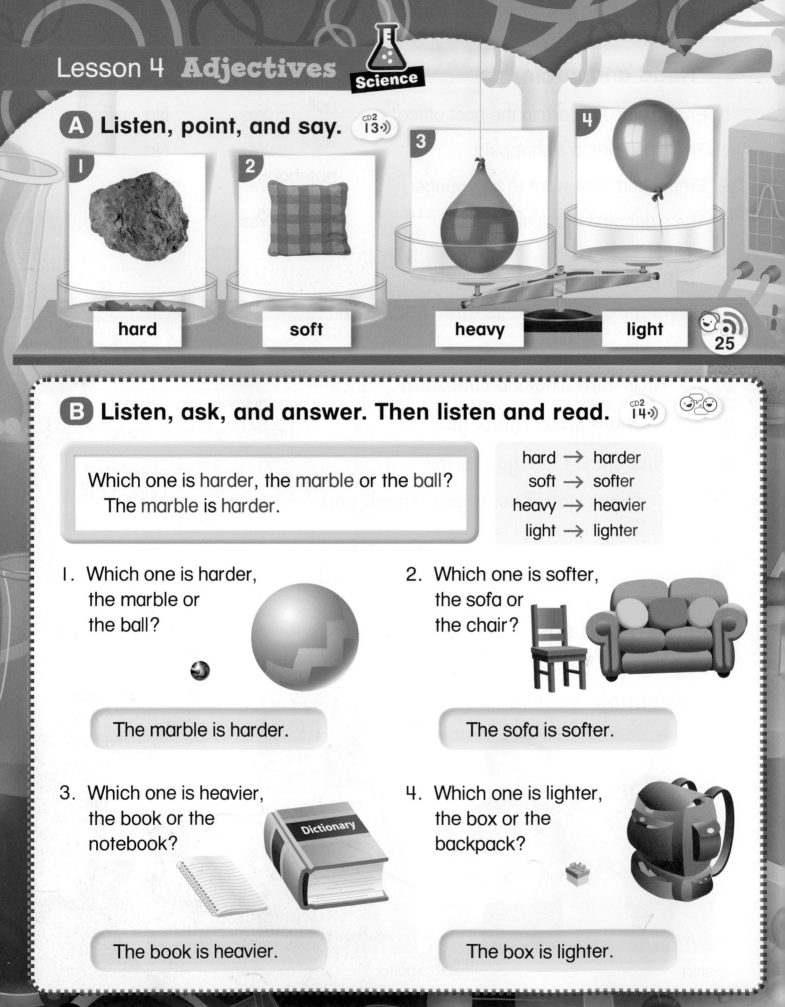

1. hard
2. soft
3. heavy
4. light

25

B Listen, ask, and answer. Then listen and read. CD2 14

Which one is harder, the marble or the ball?
  The marble is harder.

hard → harder
soft → softer
heavy → heavier
light → lighter

1. Which one is harder, the marble or the ball?

   The marble is harder.

2. Which one is softer, the sofa or the chair?

   The sofa is softer.

3. Which one is heavier, the book or the notebook?

   Dictionary

   The book is heavier.

4. Which one is lighter, the box or the backpack?

   The box is lighter.

C Read and circle.

1. Which one is softer?   marble   ball
2. Which one is harder?   chair   sofa
3. Which one is lighter?   book   notebook
4. Which one is heavier?   box   backpack

D Fill in the charts.

peach   plate

pencil   sweater

Hard	Soft

elephant   flower

potato chips   rock

Heavy	Light

E Look at at D.
Ask and answer.

Which one is softer,
the peach or the plate?

The peach is softer.

Is your backpack
heavier than your
friend's backpack?

6 Helping Out

Lesson 1 | Chores

A Listen, point, and say. CD2 15 🔊

1	2	3	4	5	6
make my bed	clean my room	do laundry	walk the dog	set the table	wash the dishes

26

B Listen and find. CD2 16 🔊

My Day

School

My Day

School

C Listen and say. Then practice. CD2 17

I make my bed before school.

before school   after school

1. 6:30 A.M.
2. 7:30 P.M.
3. 8:00 P.M.
4. 7:30 A.M.
5. 7:45 A.M.
6. 8:15 P.M.

D Listen, ask, and answer. Then practice. CD2 18

| When does | he
she | make | his
her | bed? |

| He
She | makes | his
her | bed before school. |

Before School

1.
2.
3.

After School

4.
5.
6.

E Look at B. Point, ask, and answer.

When do you clean your room?

I clean my room after school.

When do you do your homework?

Lesson 2 Chores

A Listen, point, and say. CD2 19

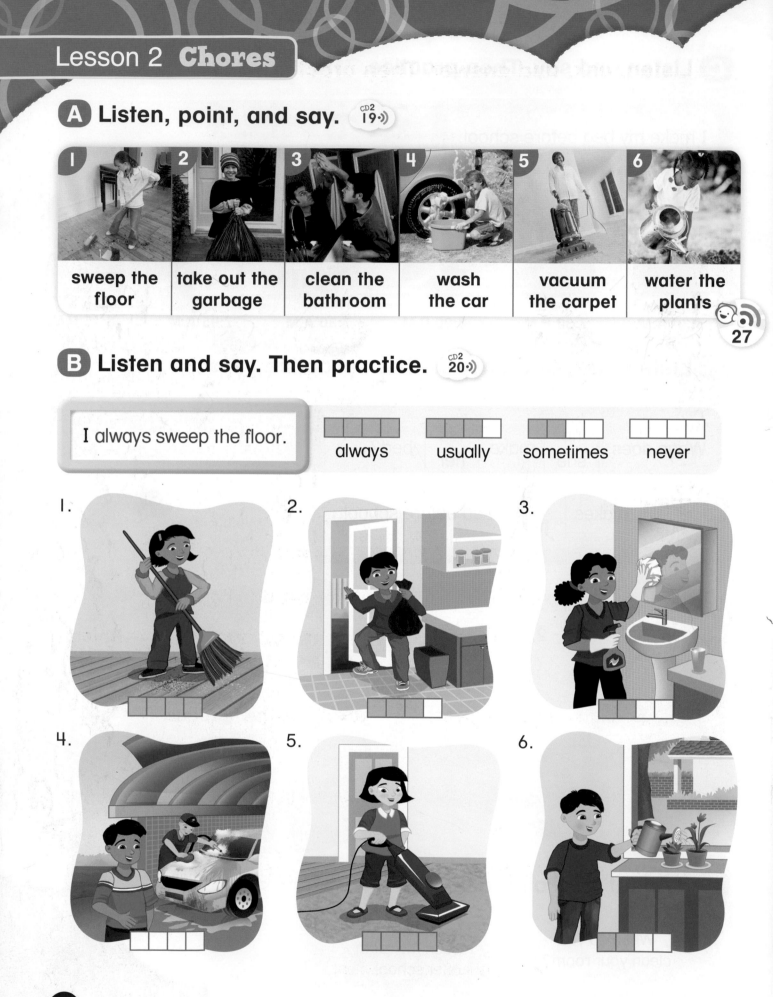

1	2	3	4	5	6
sweep the floor	take out the garbage	clean the bathroom	wash the car	vacuum the carpet	water the plants

27

B Listen and say. Then practice. CD2 20

I always sweep the floor.

always   usually   sometimes   never

1.

2.

3.

4.

5.

6.

C Listen, ask, and answer. Then practice. CD2 21))

What are	his / her	chores?	He / She	always sweeps the floor.

Emily

1.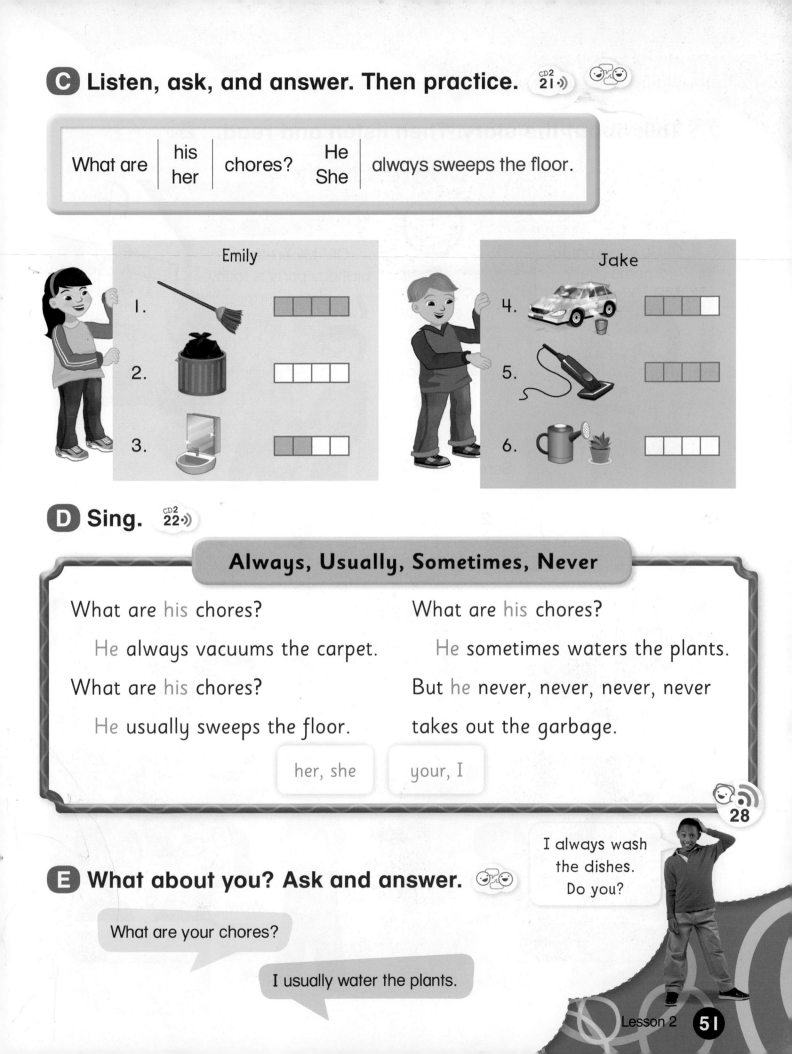

2.

3.

Jake

4.

5.

6.

D Sing. CD2 22))

Always, Usually, Sometimes, Never

What are his chores?

    He always vacuums the carpet.

What are his chores?

    He usually sweeps the floor.

What are his chores?

    He sometimes waters the plants.

But he never, never, never, never

takes out the garbage.

her, she   your, I

28

E What about you? Ask and answer.

I always wash the dishes. Do you?

What are your chores?

I usually water the plants.

A **Talk about the story. Then listen and read.** CD2 23

B Read and circle.

1. Danny wants to come over.   Yes   No
2. It's Mike's birthday.   Yes   No
3. Mike and Danny help at the party.   Yes   No
4. Leo's friend is jumping rope.   Yes   No

C Sing. CD2 24

Come Over

Do you want to come over?   Do you want to come over?

Sure. When?   Sure. When?

After school. Cool!   After school.

On Saturday. OK!   At eight. Great!

29

D Listen and say. Then act. CD2 25

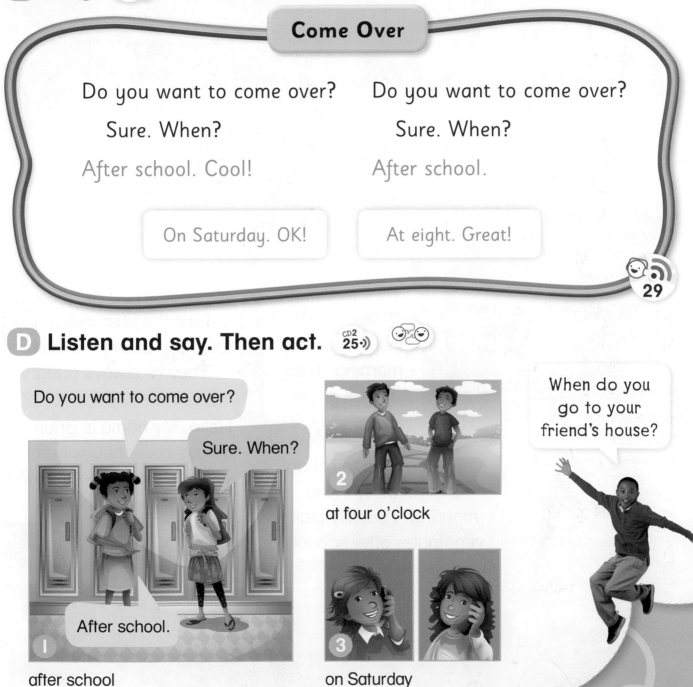

Do you want to come over?

Sure. When?

After school.

1 after school

2 at four o'clock

3 on Saturday

When do you go to your friend's house?

Lesson 4 **Farm Chores**

Social Studies

A Listen, point, and say. CD2 26

1	2	3	4
milk the cows	feed the chickens	pick vegetables	collect eggs

30

B Listen and say. Then listen and read. CD2 27

I always milk the cows	in the morning. before school.

1 Hi, I'm Vicky. I always milk the cows in the morning. Their milk is great!

2 My name is Luke. I always feed the chickens in the morning and in the evening. They're always hungry!

3 I'm Maria. I go to school at eight thirty in the morning. I usually pick vegetables after school.

4 Hello. My name is Brian. I always collect eggs before school. I do my homework in the afternoon.

C Read and circle.

1. Vicky feeds the cows in the morning.   Yes   No
2. The chickens are tired in the morning.   Yes   No
3. Maria goes to school in the evening.   Yes   No
4. Brian collects eggs before school.   Yes   No

D Listen. Fill in the chart. CD2 28

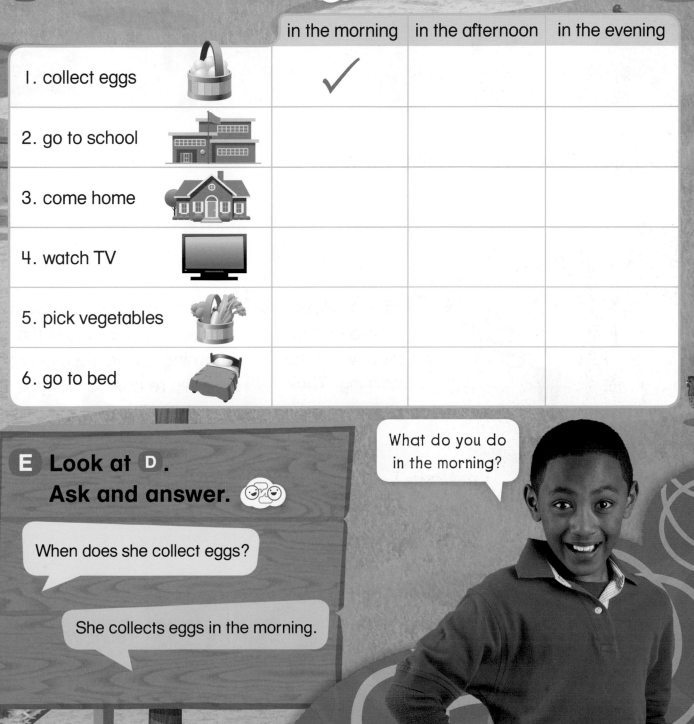

	in the morning	in the afternoon	in the evening
1. collect eggs	✓		
2. go to school			
3. come home			
4. watch TV			
5. pick vegetables			
6. go to bed			

E Look at D.
Ask and answer.

What do you do in the morning?

When does she collect eggs?

She collects eggs in the morning.

Review 3

A I can say these words.

1.
2.
3.
4.
5.
6.
7.
8.
9.
10.
11.
12.

B I can talk about these topics.

1.
2.
3.

adjectives   chores   farm chores

C I can talk with you.

1.

Thank you.

2.

Sure. When?

A Listen and read. (CD2 29)

Saturday Chores

I'm Laura, and this is my family. We always clean our house on Saturdays. I water the plants. My father washes the car. My mother sweeps the floor. My brother takes out the garbage. It's heavy, but he's strong!

B Read and answer.

1. What is Laura's chore?   _____

2. When does Laura's father wash the car?   _____

3. What is her mother's chore?   _____

4. Is the garbage heavy or light?   _____

C Listen and number. (CD2 30)

7 Out and About

A Listen, point, and say. CD2 31

1	2	3	4	5	6
beach	aquarium	amusement park	museum	hotel	pool

B Listen and find. CD2 32

C Listen, ask, and answer. Then practice. CD2 33

| Where was | he
she | yesterday? | He
She | was at the beach. |

	Sunday	Monday
	1	2
	yesterday	today

1. 2. 3. 4. 5. 6.

D Listen, ask, and answer. Then practice. CD2 34

| Was | he
she | at the beach yesterday? |

| Yes, | he | was. | He | was at the aquarium. |
| No, | she | wasn't. | She | |

wasn't = was not

I was at the pool on Saturday.

E Look at **B**. Point, ask, and answer.

Where was he?

He was at the aquarium.

A Listen, point, and say. CD2 35

1	2	3	4	5	6
bookstore	pharmacy	toy store	hair salon	coffee shop	flower shop

32

B Listen, ask, and answer. Then practice. CD2 36

> Where were they yesterday?   They were at the bookstore.

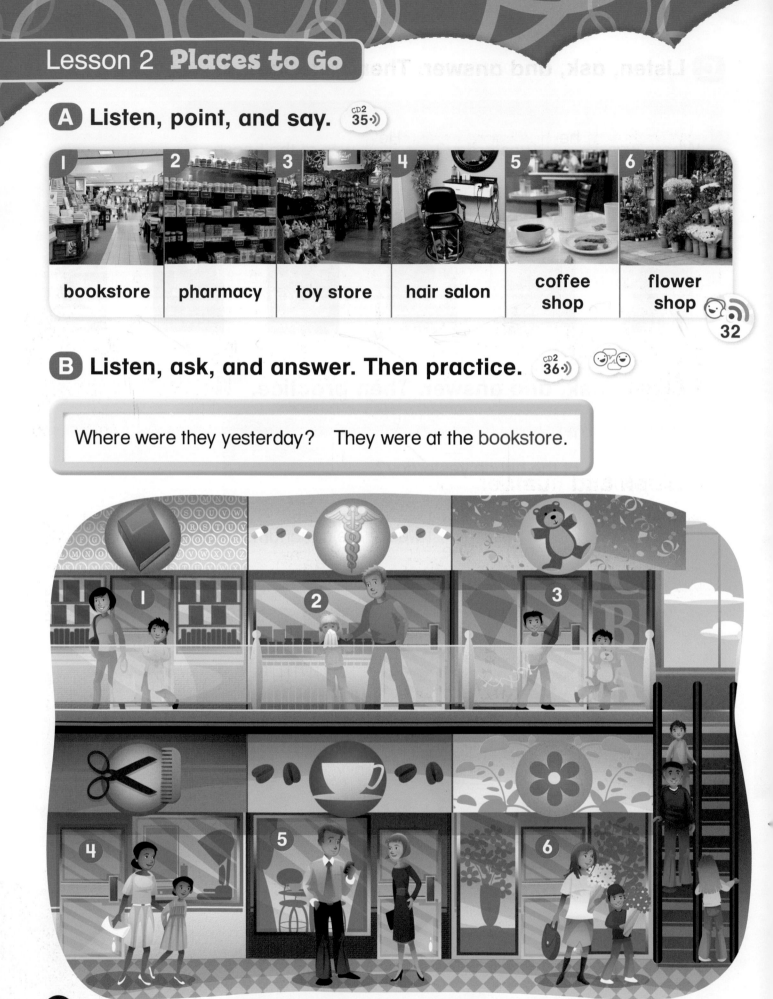

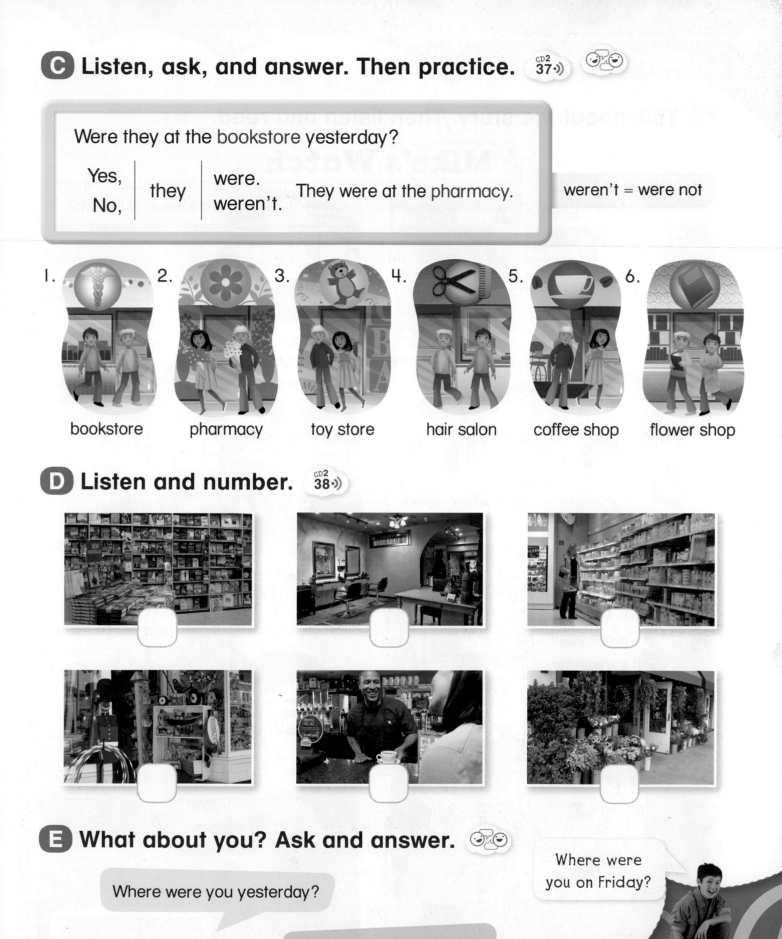

C **Listen, ask, and answer. Then practice.** CD2 37

Were they at the bookstore yesterday?

| Yes, | they | were. | They were at the pharmacy. |
| No, | | weren't. | |

weren't = were not

1. bookstore
2. pharmacy
3. toy store
4. hair salon
5. coffee shop
6. flower shop

D **Listen and number.** CD2 38

E **What about you? Ask and answer.**

Where were you yesterday?

Where were you on Friday?

I was at the flower shop.

A **Talk about the story. Then listen and read.** CD2 39

B Read and circle.

1. The class is at the aquarium.   Yes   No
2. Mike and Danny want ice cream.   Yes   No
3. The boys are on time.   Yes   No
4. Mike needs a new watch.   Yes   No

C Sing. CD2 40

See You Then

Let's meet here before school.

OK. See you then.

See you at seven fifteen.

OK. Be on time.

in the afternoon
one o'clock

at five o'clock
five o'clock

33

D Listen and say. Then act. CD2 41

Let's meet here at five o'clock.

OK. See you then.

1

five o'clock

2

twelve thirty

3

six forty-five

Do you have
a watch?

Lesson 4 Weather

Science

A Listen, point, and say. CD2 42

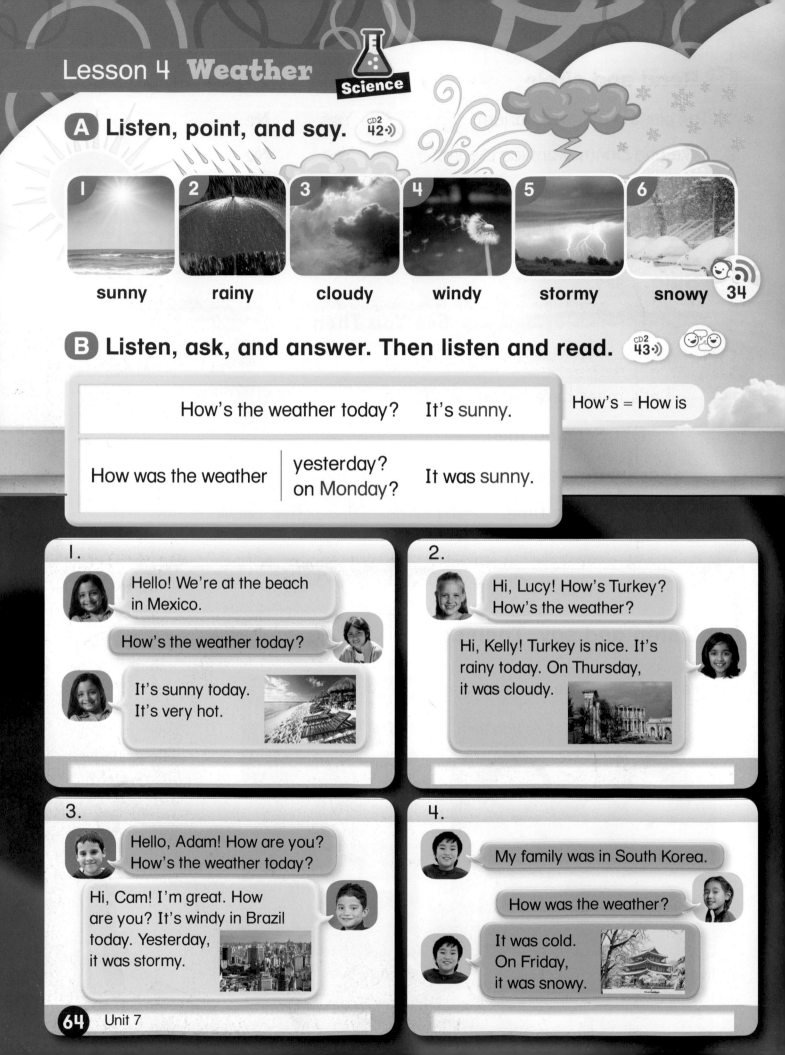

1. sunny
2. rainy
3. cloudy
4. windy
5. stormy
6. snowy

34

B Listen, ask, and answer. Then listen and read. CD2 43

How's the weather today?   It's sunny.

How's = How is

| How was the weather | yesterday? on Monday? | It was sunny. |

1.
Hello! We're at the beach in Mexico.

How's the weather today?

It's sunny today. It's very hot.

2.
Hi, Lucy! How's Turkey? How's the weather?

Hi, Kelly! Turkey is nice. It's rainy today. On Thursday, it was cloudy.

3.
Hello, Adam! How are you? How's the weather today?

Hi, Cam! I'm great. How are you? It's windy in Brazil today. Yesterday, it was stormy.

4.
My family was in South Korea.

How was the weather?

It was cold. On Friday, it was snowy.

C Read and circle.

1. It's sunny today in Mexico.   Yes   No
2. It was snowy in Turkey on Thursday.   Yes   No
3. It was sunny in Brazil yesterday.   Yes   No
4. It was snowy in South Korea.   Yes   No

D Make a weather chart. Draw and write.

Sunday	Monday	Tuesday	Wednesday	Thursday	Friday	Saturday

How's the weather today?

E Look at D. Ask and answer.

How was the weather on Monday?

It was sunny on Monday.

8 Things We Use

Lesson 1 | School Supplies

A Listen, point, and say. CD2 44»)

1	2	3	4	5	6
folder	lunchbox	water bottle	dictionary	calculator	stapler

35

B Listen and find. CD2 45»)

Yesterday Morning

C Listen, ask, and answer. Then practice. CD2 46

Where was the folder?   It was on the table.

After

Before

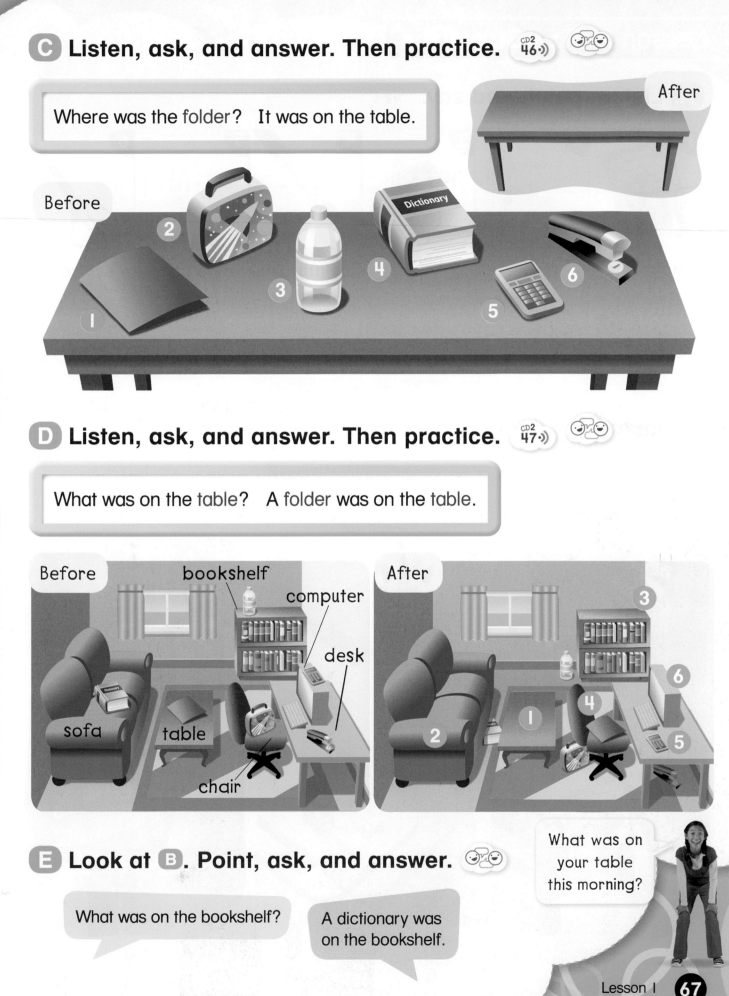

D Listen, ask, and answer. Then practice. CD2 47

What was on the table?   A folder was on the table.

Before

bookshelf
computer
desk
sofa
table
chair

After

E Look at B. Point, ask, and answer.

What was on the bookshelf?

A dictionary was on the bookshelf.

What was on your table this morning?

A Listen, point, and say. CD2 48·))

1	2	3	4	5	6
magazine	poster	pencil sharpener	paintbrush	glue stick	scissors

36

B Listen and say. Then practice. CD2 49·))

There	were some / weren't any	magazines on the table.

magazines   posters
pencil sharpeners paint brushes
glue sticks   scissors

weren't = were not

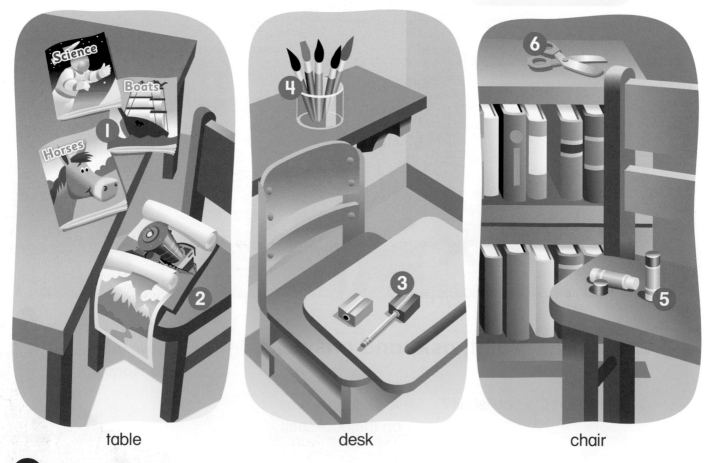

table   desk   chair

C Listen, ask, and answer. Then practice. CD2 50

Were there any magazines on the table?	Yes,	there	were.
	No,		weren't.

1.
table

2.
computer

3.
table

4.
chair

5.
Alphabet
Aa Bb Cc Dd
Ed Ff Gg Hh Ii
Jj Kk Ll Mm Nn
Oo Pp Qq Rr Ss
Tt Uu Vv Ww
Xx Yy Zz
PLANETS
Recycle
wall

6.
desk

D Sing. CD2 51

Were There Any?

Were there any glue sticks on the bookshelf?
　　Yes, there were some glue sticks on the bookshelf.
Were there any glue sticks on the wall?
　　No, there weren't any glue sticks on the wall.
They were on the bookshelf.

scissors
desk

paintbrushes
table

37

E Ask and answer about your bedroom.

There were paintbrushes on the desk. Where are they now?

Were there any scissors on the table?

Yes, there were.

A Talk about the story. Then listen and read.

B Read and circle.

1.	Emma and Julie were at the beach.	Yes	No
2.	The river was dirty.	Yes	No
3.	There were flowers everywhere.	Yes	No
4.	Emma asks how to spell "Saturday."	Yes	No

C Sing. CD2 53

How Do You Spell?

How do you spell Saturday?

How do you spell Saturday?

How do you spell... How do you spell...

How do you spell Saturday?

S-A-T-U-R-D-A-Y.

magazine

your name

38

D Listen and say. Then act. CD2 54

How do you spell "Saturday"?

S-A-T-U-R-D-A-Y.

2

3

How was your day today?

Lesson 4 Technology

Social Studies

A Listen, point, and say. CD2 55

1	2	3	4
cell phone	laptop	digital TV	digital camera

39

B Listen and say. Then listen and read. CD2 56

There weren't any cell phones in 1940. There were phones like this.

1. There weren't any cell phones in 1940. Phones were bigger and heavier. There were phones like this.

2. There weren't any laptops in 1960. Computers were bigger and noisier. There were computers like this.

3. There weren't any digital TVs in 1955. TVs were smaller. The pictures were in black and white. There were TVs like this.

4. There weren't any digital cameras in 1915. Cameras were slower and bigger. There were cameras like this.

C Read and circle.

1. There were cell phones in 1940.   Yes   No

2. Computers were bigger and noisier in 1960.   Yes   No

3. There were TVs in 1955.   Yes   No

4. Cameras were faster and smaller in 1915.   Yes   No

D Look at at B. Fill in the timeline.

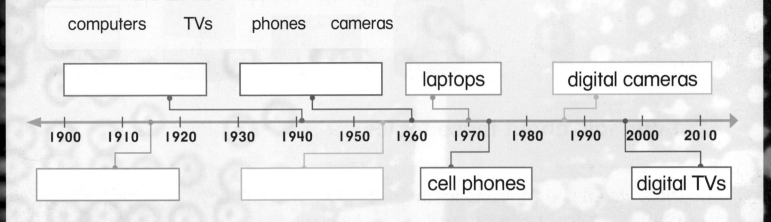

computers   TVs   phones   cameras

laptops   digital cameras

1900   1910   1920   1930   1940   1950   1960   1970   1980   1990   2000   2010

cell phones   digital TVs

E Look at at D. Ask and answer.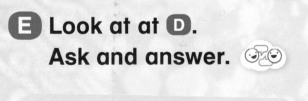

Were there laptops before 2000?

Yes, there were.

Were there laptops in 1960?

No, there weren't.

Do you have a cell phone?

Review 4

A I can say these words.

1. 2. 3. 4. 5. 6.

7. 8. 9. 10. 11. 12.

B I can talk about these topics.

1.

places to go

2.

the weather

3.

school supplies

4.

art supplies

5.

technology

C I can talk with you.

1.

Let's meet here at five o'clock.

2.

S-C-I-S-S-O-R-S.

A Listen and read. CD2 57

Troy's Day

I'm Troy. Yesterday, it was sunny and hot. I was at the beach with my family. There were big hotels and an aquarium. There was an amusement park, too. It was fun.

ADMIT ONE
910973 91097
ADMIT ONE
910973 910973

B Read and circle.

1. How was the weather yesterday? sunny cloudy
2. Where was Troy? at the beach at the park
3. Were they cold? Yes, they were. No, they weren't.
4. Was there an aquarium? Yes, there was. No, there wasn't.

C Listen and number. CD2 58

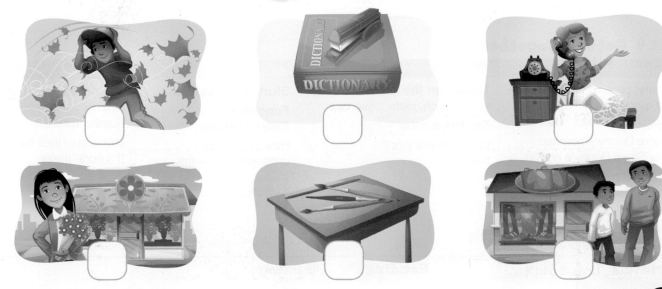

Syllabus

Unit 1 Things to Eat

Lesson 1	Lesson 2	Lesson 3	Lesson 4
Snacks: gum, popcorn, peanuts, chocolate, potato chips, soda I want some / don't want any gum. He / She wants some / doesn't want any gum. What do you want? I want some gum. What does he / she want? He / She wants some gum.	**Vegetables:** carrot, onion, pepper, cabbage, potato, tomato Do you need any carrots? Yes, we do. No, we don't. What do they need? They need a carrot / some carrots.	**Story: Just Try It** **Functional Conversation:** What's for lunch? Soup and salad. That sounds good. `Be healthy.`	**Cooking:** omelet, smoothie, fruit salad, milkshake I want to make an omelet. *Health*

Unit 2 Around Town

Lesson 1	Lesson 2	Lesson 3	Lesson 4
Places to Go: park, movie theater, supermarket, post office, department store, library Where's the park? It's across from the movie theater. It's between the school and the movie theater.	**Things to Do:** shop, watch a movie, borrow books, mail letters, buy groceries, kick a ball What's he / she doing at the department store? He's / She's shopping.	**Story: It's Over There!** **Functional Conversation:** Excuse me. Where's the post office? It's over there. `Be helpful.`	**Activities:** color, cut, glue, fold First, color the house. *Art*

Review 1 Units 1 and 2   **Reading** Movie Day

Unit 3 People in Town

Lesson 1	Lesson 2	Lesson 3	Lesson 4
Occupations: cashier, librarian, postal worker, salesperson, server, vet Who works at the supermarket? Where does the cashier work? The cashier works at the supermarket.	**What People Do:** make food, sell things, help sick animals, drive buses, fly planes, fight fires What does the cook do? The cook makes food. Does the cook make food / sell things? Yes, he / she does. No, he / she doesn't.	**Story: Mom's Present** **Functional Conversation:** Excuse me. How much is this sweater? It's $30. `Be thoughtful.`	**Illnesses:** cold, fever, stomachache, headache What's the matter with him / her? He / She has a cold. *Health*

Unit 4 Getting Together

Lesson 1	Lesson 2	Lesson 3	Lesson 4
Family: parents, grandparents, aunt, uncle, cousin (m), cousin (f) They're Danny's parents. He's / She's Danny's cousin. Who are they? They're his / her parents. Who's he / she? He's his / her uncle. She's his / her aunt.	**Things on the Table:** fork, knife, spoon, plate, bowl, cup This fork is mine. Whose fork is that? It's mine.	**Story: Chopsticks** **Functional Conversation:** How do you use chopsticks? Like this. `Be helpful.`	**Countries:** Mexico, Japan, Russia, Turkey This is our / their flag. It's ours / theirs. *Social Studies*

Review 2 Units 3 and 4   **Reading** Our Presents

Unit 5 Fun in the Park

Lesson 1	Lesson 2	Lesson 3	Lesson 4
Adjectives: tall/short, old/young, strong/weak, girl, boy, woman, man The girl is tall. The boy is taller. Who's taller, Danny or Julie? Danny is taller.	**Adjectives:** thick, thin, clean, dirty, pretty, ugly The red socks are thicker than the blue socks. Is the red sweater thicker/thinner than the blue sweater? Yes, it is. No, it isn't.	**Story: Cool Shirt** **Functional Conversation:** Nice shirt! Thank you. Be nice.	**Adjectives:** hard, soft, heavy, light Which one is harder, the marble or the ball? The marble is harder.

Unit 6 Helping Out

Lesson 1	Lesson 2	Lesson 3	Lesson 4
Chores: make my bed, clean my room, do laundry, walk the dog, set the table, wash the dishes I make my bed before school. When does he/she make his/her bed? He/She makes his/her bed before school.	**Chores:** sweep the floor, take out the garbage, clean the bathroom, wash the car, vacuum the carpet, water the plants I always sweep the floor. What are his/her chores? He/She always sweeps the floor.	**Story: Come Over** **Functional Conversation:** Do you want to come over? Sure. When? After school. Be friendly.	**Farm Chores:** milk the cows, feed the chickens, pick vegetables, collect eggs I always milk the cows in the morning/before school.

Review 3 Units 5 and 6   **Reading**   Saturday Chores

Unit 7 Out and About

Lesson 1	Lesson 2	Lesson 3	Lesson 4
Places to Go: beach, aquarium, amusement park, museum, hotel, pool Where was he/she yesterday? He/She was at the beach. Was he/she at the beach yesterday? Yes, he/she was. No, he/she wasn't. He/She was at the aquarium.	**Places to Go:** bookstore, pharmacy, toy store, hair salon, coffee shop, flower shop Where were they yesterday? They were at the bookstore. Were they at the bookstore yesterday? Yes, they were. No, they weren't. They were at the pharmacy.	**Story: Mike's Watch** **Functional Conversation:** Let's meet here at five o'clock. OK. See you then. Be on time.	**Weather:** sunny, rainy, cloudy, windy, stormy, snowy How's the weather today? It's sunny. How was the weather yesterday/on Monday? It was sunny.

Unit 8 Things We Use

Lesson 1	Lesson 2	Lesson 3	Lesson 4
School Supplies: folder, lunchbox, water bottle, dictionary, calculator, stapler Where was the folder? It was on the table. What was on the table? A folder was on the table.	**Art Supplies:** magazine, poster, pencil sharpener, paintbrush, glue stick, scissors There were some/weren't any magazines on the table. Were there any magazines on the table? Yes, there were./ No, there weren't.	**Story: Let's Clean Up!** **Functional Conversation:** How do you spell "Saturday"? S-A-T-U-R-D-A-Y. Be helpful.	**Technology:** cell phone, laptop, digital TV, digital camera There weren't any cell phones in 1940. There were phones like this.

Review 4 Units 7 and 8   **Reading**   Troy's Day

Syllabus   **77**

Word List